WANTON LOVERBOY

KALEVALA 1835-1985

WANTON LOVERBOY

KALEVALA cantos 11—15

Translated by
Keith Bosley

FINNISH
LITERATURE SOCIETY
Helsinki

Finnish
Literature Society
Editions 416

ISBN 951-717-394-6
ISSN 0355-1768

Typesetting by Fraktuura Oy, Helsinki
Printed in Finland by
Sisälähetysseuran kirjapaino Raamattutalo, Pieksämäki 1985

Contents

To the Reader

The section of the *Kalevala* translated here
inspired the well-known group of tone-poems by
Sibelius known variously as *Four Legends* and
the *Lemminkäinen Suite,* Op22. They celebrate
their hero's cavortings with the maidens of Saari
('the Island'), the swan of Tuonela (the abode
of the dead), Lemminkäinen's unhappy sojourn
there, and his miraculous return. It seems
appropriate to invoke Sibelius thus as the outset
of the present work, since for most English
speakers he is the chief way into the strange
world of the *Kalevala*.

Lemminkäinen the 'wanton Loverboy', alias
Ahti the Islander, alias Farmind: of the *Kalevala*
characters he is the most vividly portrayed — a
young man who plays fast and loose with
women and with men who get in his way. His
clutch of names points to a composite figure
based on a number of characters in Finnish
myth: so who is — or was — Lemminkäinen?

For perhaps two millennia until its death just
within living memory, one of the richest oral
traditions known flourished in the eastern Baltic
area among nations whose linguistic ancestry
has been traced to a group of tribes who had
migrated from north-east European Russia. By
far the biggest of these nations, the Finns,

absorbed influences from their Baltic and Germanic as well as their Slav neighbours, and it was this meeting of cultures which gave the Finnish tradition its exceptional vitality.

From the late 18th century into the early 20th Finnish scholars travelled the wilds of their country collecting from unlettered singers the epic tales, the lyrics, the spells, laments and proverbs which Christianity had failed to stamp out but which were finally losing ground to material progress. In 1809 this province of Sweden became a Grand Duchy of Russia, but as the century advanced the Finns became increasingly aware of their identity as a nation. This awareness was stimulated in no small part by the labours of one of the collectors, the country doctor Elias Lönnrot (1802—84), who edited and arranged much of his material to form two monumental works, the epic *Kalevala* (first edition 1835) and the treasury of lyrics *Kanteletar* (1840); the second and definitive edition of the *Kalevala* (1849) is, at 22795 lines, roughly twice the size of its predecessor.

The section translated here, cantos 11—15 of fifty in all, forms about one-tenth of the epic. It introduces Lemminkäinen, who snatches Kyllikki from her Island and marries her; she agrees not to go gallivanting as long as he does not go to war. She misinterprets his absence on a fishing trip and breaks the agreement, whereupon he abandons her to woo the Maid of the North, known to music-lovers as Pohjola's Daughter (Pohjola means Northland). Her mother sets him three tasks to prove his worth — to capture the Demon's elk, then the Demon's horse, and finally to shoot the swan on the river of Tuonela. He completes the first two tasks, but is murdered while attempting the third. On learning this, his mother restores him to life by magic and whisks him off home.

The *Kalevala* consists of thousands of fragments assembled into a continuous narrative. An idea of Lönnrot's method can be gained by looking at the kind of material that went into this sequence. Finnish folk poetry is well documented: for a start there is the 33-volume *Old Poems of the Finnish People*

(Suomen Kansan Vanhat Runot, in Finnish only) and its one-volume offspring *Finnish Folk Poetry: Epic* (in Finnish and English).

In *Epic* we find two poems (Nos 39 and 40) about a bond between a certain Ahti and his bride Kyllikki, which he breaks. Both poems were collected in Karelia, and seem to belong to the Eastern Viking branch of the Finnish tradition: Ahti is a footloose Viking. Poem 34 tells of a fight in which Ahti cuts off Lemminkäinen's head 'like cropping a turnip'; but in the *Kalevala* Ahti is no more than one aspect of Lemminkäinen, who will be cropping someone else's head in a later episode. Poem 35 tells of Lemminkäinen the gatecrasher, barred from a feast because of his incest with his sister — a crime which Lönnrot in the *Kalevala* transfers to Kullervo. He boasts to his mother beforehand that if he comes to grief his hairbrush at home will ooze blood, and he speaks memorably to her afterwards as a drowned man: these details go into our sequence with its different story, and the gatecrashing story forms a later canto. While both Lemminkäinen and Ahti are credited in the tradition with magical powers, the shamanistic aspect may be more apparent in the *Kalevala* character's third name, Kaukomieli. In Karelia in 1834 Lönnrot himself collected a poem about one Kaukamieli from Arhippa Perttunen, one of the greatest singers: this poem, No.37 in *Epic,* reveals most of the character we recognise, at whose departure 'the brides of the Island wept'. Finnish *mieli* means both mind and inclination: does the name therefore mean far-inclined, ambitious or proud? Or does it mean someone whose mind can range far, whose spirit has wings, a shaman? The present translation has settled for Farmind. Much else has gone into our sequence: it is a tribute to Lönnrot's genius that the story he has constructed is so coherent and so compelling.

The text offered here is part of work in progress and hence subject to change and open to suggestion: a complete translation of the *Kalevala* will be published in the Oxford University Press World's Classics series towards the end of the decade. The main problem for the translator is making a credible sound where there is no cultural equivalent: oral tradition, in which the *Kalevala* is rooted, is central to Finnish culture but peripheral to English. Since the days of *Piers Plowman* our poets have written and signed their work, while their Finnish contemporaries remained mute inglorious Miltons until the Romantic movement gave them to their nation and to the world: it is as though English literature had developed from Percy's *Reliques*.

Faced with the *Kalevala* and its parent tradition, the English translator has responded in three ways: let us take them chronologically, and focus on the rendering of a key word, which occurs five times in canto 12 — *tietäjä*, literally 'knower', one who knows things not generally known. The first two translators, the American John Martin Crawford (1889, working from Schiefner's German version) and the Englishman William Forsell Kirby (1907) responded as Chapman the Elizabethan did to Homer: they assumed a cultural equivalent. Chapman's Homer (beloved of Keats) is in ballad metre; Crawford and Kirby, following the example of Goethe's *Finnisches Lied* (a translation of a folk lyric), Schiefner's *Kalevala* and Longfellow's *Hiawatha* (inspired by the *Kalevala)*, used the basic form of the original metre — four trochees ('with their frequent repetitions'). But there is far more to Kalevala metre than that, and their versions trot where the original dances. As for *tietäjä,* Crawford has 'wizard', Kirby has 'minstrel': Crawford, though etymologically impeccable, patronises, while Kirby romanticises. Another American, Francis Peabody Magoun Jr (1963), assumes no cultural equivalent and makes a virtue of not doing so. His liberal conscience demanded a plain prose rendering, which might interest anthropologists, but hardly appeals to the ordinary reader of poetry: one meets people (including the present writer) who have been captivated by Kirby, but never by Magoun. His rendering of *tietäjä* is better, but the scholarly overtones of 'sage' (the Romance counterpart of the Frankish wizard) accord ill with the homespun original. The present translator, like Magoun, knows that English literature has nothing like the *Kalevala,* but proceeds to fill the gap by invention. By its very nature, language excommunicates more than it communicates, and translation can never do more than mediate, and the best mediator is the least noticed. He avoids both jumping to conclusions and despairing of any: he must build a bridge and then disappear. The present syllable-based metre, arrived at through translating the poems of *Epic* and a great deal besides, is offered as such a bridge, across which *tietäjä* becomes 'wise man', like the astrologers in the King James version of the Gospel or their female colleagues who made concoctions of healing English herbs.

The translation in progress is being made direct from the original into what it is hoped is English verse, with not too much help from previous translators. Lönnrot's summaries at the head of each canto have been replaced by titles. Among works of reference, the *Kalevalan Sanat* ('Words of the *Kalevala')* of Aimo Turunen is indispensable. Senni Timonen is contributing priceless insights. Satu Salo is combining the role of first critic with those of musician, wife and mother. With such help, shortcomings can only be blamed on the translator.

Upton-cum-Chalvey
October 1984   *Keith Bosley*

A Bond Made

'Tis time to tell of Ahti
and to lilt about a rogue.

Ahti the Islander boy
he the wanton Loverboy
grew up in a lofty home
   with his dear mother
at the broadest bay's far end
underneath Far Headland's arm.

On fish there Farmind grew up
on perch Ahti rose up tall
became a man of the best
a red-blooded one burst forth
   who has a good head
   and can hold his own;
but he went a little wrong
   fell into bad ways:
he hung around with women
   he stayed out all night
making merry with the girls
capering with braided heads.

Kylli was an Island maid
an Island maid, Island flower.

She grew in a lofty home
rose up in a graceful one
sitting in her father's rooms
lounging upon the back bench.

Long she grew, widely was famed:
    suitors came from far
    to the maid's famous
    home, to her fair farm.

The sun wooed her for his son:
she would not go to Sunland
    to shine with the sun
    in the summer rush.

The moon wooed her for his son:
she would not go to Moonland
    to gleam with the moon
    to patrol the sky's circuits.

A star wooed her for his son:
she would not go to Starland
to twinkle throughout the nights
    in the winter skies.

From Estonia bridegrooms came
others from far Ingria:
she would not go there either;
    but she answered back:
'In vain is your gold used up
    your silver worn thin!
I'll not go to Estonia
I'll not go, nor pledge myself
to row Estonian water
    punt between islands
    eat Estonian fish
    gulp Estonian broth.

'Nor will I go to Ingria
    to its banks and braes;
there is lack, lack of all things —
lack of trees and lack of splints
lack of water, lack of wheat

and lack of rye bread.'

Well, wanton Lemminkäinen
    fair Farmind himself
    pledged that he would go
a-wooing the Island flower
    that especial bride
the beautiful braided head.

His mother tried to forbid
    the old woman warned:
    'Do not go, my son
    among your betters!
You may not be accepted
among the Island's great kin.'

Wanton Lemminkäinen said
    fair Farmind uttered:
'If my home is not handsome
and my kin not great enough
I'll choose with my manly frame
take with my other features.'

And still his mother forbids
Lemminkäinen to go off
among the Island's great kin
    its good families:
'There the lasses will taunt you
the women will abuse you.'

What did Lemminkäinen care!
He put this in words: 'Indeed
I'll ward off women's laughter
and the giggles of daughters:
I'll kick a boy at the breast
    and a babe-in-arms;
that will stop even good taunts
    better insults too.'

His mother put this in words:
'Ah, luckless me, for my days!
If you abused the Island
women, spoilt the pure lasses

a quarrel would come of it
and a great war would befall!
All the Island's great bridegrooms
a hundred men with their swords
would fall on you, luckless one
would surround you on your own.'

What did Lemminkäinen care
about his mother's warning!
He takes his good stallion, he
    harnessed his choice foal;
    and he rumbles off
to the Island's famed village
for to woo the Island flower
the Island's especial bride.

The women abused Lemminkäinen
the lasses poked fun, for he
drove oddly along the lane
grimly into the farmyard:
he drove his sleigh till it tipped
at the gate rolled it over.

There wanton Lemminkäinen
twisted his mouth, turned his head
and twisted his black whiskers.
He himself put this in words:
'I have not seen this before
have not seen, nor have I heard
a woman abusing me
put up with a lass's taunts.'

What did Lemminkäinen care!
He uttered a word, spoke thus:
'Does the Island have somewhere
some land upon its mainland
    where I can play games
    ground where I can dance
make merry with Island girls
and caper with braided heads?'

    The Island girls say
and the headland maids answer:

'Yes, the Island has somewhere
some land upon its mainland
    where you can play games
    ground where you can dance —
clearings fit for a cowherd
burnt land fit for a herdsman:
the Island children are lean
    while the foals grow fat.'

What did Lemminkäinen care!
He found work as a herdsman
spent the days herding, the nights
making merry with the girls
    sporting with those maids
capering with braided heads.

Thus wanton Lemminkäinen
    fair Farmind himself
warded off woman's laughter
and held off a lass's taunts.
    There was no daughter
not even the purest lass
    who he did not touch
    and did not lie with.

One girl there was of them all
among the Island's great kin
who would not accept bridegrooms
    take to kind husbands:
that was handsome Kyllikki
the Island's beautiful flower.

Well, wanton Lemminkäinen
    fair Farmind himself
wore away a hundred boots
rowed a hundred oars in half
    going for this maid
    hunting Kyllikki.

Kyllikki the handsome maid
    just put this in words:
'Why, wretch, do you rush about,
croaking plover, drive about

pestering the girls from here
chatting up the tin-belted?
I shall not have time before
I have worn out the grindstone
beaten the stamper away
pounded the mortar to bits.

'I do not care for birdbrains
for birdbrains, for scatterbrains;
I want one of shapely frame
    for my shapely frame
someone with grander features
    for my grand features
someone with a fairer face
    for my own fair face.'

   A little time passed
barely half a month went by.

On a day among others
an evening among many
    the maids are sporting
the beauties are capering
on the backwoods' mainland side
    upon the fair heath;
Kyllikki above the rest
the Island's flower the most famed.

And the full-blooded rogue came
wanton Lemminkäinen drove
    with his own stallion
    with his chosen foal
into the midst of their sport
of the beauties' capers; snatched
Kyllikki into his sledge
grabbed the maid into his sleigh
    dumped her on his hide
    laid her on his planks.

   And he whipped his horse
thrashed it with his thong
then he glided off.
As he goes he says:

'Girls, do not ever
blow the gaff on me —
that I have been here
took a maid from here!'

'If you don't heed what I say
it will be the worse for you:
I'll sing your bridegrooms to war
your young men beneath the sword
so they'll be heard nevermore
nor seen ever in this world
    walking in the lanes
    driving in the glades.'

Truly Kyllikki complained
    the Island's flower wailed:
    'Release me now, give
    the child her freedom
    to go her home
back to her weeping mother!

'If you will not give me leave
    and let me go home
    my five brothers yet
my uncle's seven children
will trample on the hare's foot
will demand the maid's head back.'

When she could not anyway
escape, she burst into tears.
She uttered a word, spoke thus:
'For nothing was I, luckless one, born
for nothing was born, for nothing grew
for nothing I lived my time;
now I end up with a good-
for-nothing, a worthless man
in care of a warmonger
a harsh one always fighting!'

Wanton Lemminkäinen said
    fair Farmind uttered:
'Kyllikki my heartsease, my
sweet-tasting little berry!

Don't worry at all!
I may not treat you badly —
you in my arms as I eat
you in my hands as I walk
you at my side as I stand
you beside me as I lie.

   'So why do you grieve
why do you sigh full of care?
   Is this why you grieve
and why you sigh full of care —
that you'll have no cows, no bread
and little to call your own?

   'Don't worry at all!
   I have many cows
   many milk givers:
first on the swamp there is Buttercup
then on the hill there is Strawberry
and third Cowberry in the clearing.
Not eating, they are handsome
not looked after, they are fine;
there's no evening tethering
and no morning letting out
no tossing of a hay-bale
no worry for salt or feed.

   'Or else is this why you grieve
and why you sigh full of care —
that my kinsfolk are not great
my home not very lofty?

   'Though I am not great of kin
     nor lofty of home
     my sword is fiery
my iron blade is sparkling.
   Here's what great kin is
   and a mighty clan —
being refined among demons
   polished among gods.
Here's how I make my kin great
   all my clan mighty —
with a sword of fiery edge

with a sparkling brand.'

The hapless maid sighs
herself put this into words:
'Alas, Ahti, Loverboy!
If you want a maid like me
for an everlasting spouse
for a hen under your arm
you, swear everlasting oaths
that you will not go to war —
not even for need of gold
even for greed of silver!'

There wanton Lemminkäinen
himself put this into words:
'I swear everlasting oaths
that I shall not go to war —
not even for need of gold
even for greed of silver.
Now you, swear your oath that you
will not go to the village —
not for greed of a good hop
even, for need of a dance!'

Thereupon they swore their oaths
made their pledges for ever
before the God known to all
beneath the almighty's face;
Ahti would not go to war
Kyllikki to the village.

Then wanton Lemminkäinen
    lashed the courser on
smote the stallion with the rein
himself put this into words:
    'Farewell, Island turfs
    spruce roots, tarry stumps
where I have walked in summer
    tramped all the winters
lurking upon cloudy nights
and fleeing in bad weather
as I was hunting this grouse
and chasing the long-tailed duck!'

He canters away;
   soon his home appears.
The maid put this into words
herself declared and spoke thus:
'A cabin is looming there
a lean hovel appearing.
   Whose is that cabin
whose is that ne'er-do-well's home?'

That wanton Lemminkäinen
uttered a word and spoke thus:
'Don't you grieve about cabins
   don't sigh about huts!
Other cabins may be built
better ones may be put up
   with enormous beams
   and with the best joists.'

Then wanton Lemminkäinen
   quickly arrives home
   to his dear mother
beside his honoured parent.

His mother put this in words
herself declared and spoke thus:
'You have tarried long, my son
   long in foreign lands.'

Wanton Lemminkäinen said
uttered a word and spoke thus:
   'I had to abuse
the women, avenge the pure lasses
because they kept taunting me
   kept abusing me.
I got the best in my sleigh
   dumped her on my hide
   laid her on my planks
and beneath the quilt rolled her.
Thus I paid the women for abuse
the lasses for making fun.

'O my mother who bore me

my mamma who brought me up!
What I set out for I got
and what I hunted I caught.
Lay now your best mattresses
   your softest pillows
for me in my own land to
   lie with my young maid!'

His mother put this in words
herself declared and chattered:
   'Be praised now, O God,
exalted, O Lord, alone,
for giving me a daughter-in-law
bringing a good fire-blower
an excellent cloth-weaver
a most capable spinner
a first-class washerwoman
   and bleacher of clothes!

   'And you, thank your luck!
Good you got and good you found
good your Creator promised
good the merciful one gave:
pure is the bunting on snow
purer is the one you have;
white on the sea is the foam
whiter is the one you hold;
sweet on the sea is the duck
sweeter is the one you keep;
bright is the star in the sky
brighter is the one you wed.

'Prepare floors now that are wide
get windows that are bigger
raise walls that are new, and build
a whole cabin that's better
thresholds before the cabin
and new doors at the threshold
because you have a young maid
and have picked out a fair one
   one better than you
     greater than your kin!'

A Bond Broken

Then Ahti Lemminkäinen
he the fair faraway man
continued living his time
   with the young maiden;
he did not go to war, nor
Kyllikki to the village.

On a day among others
a morning among many
he, Ahti Lemminkäinen
went off to catch fish spawning
did not come home at evening
for the first night stayed away.
So Kyllikki went to the village
to sport with the young maidens.

   Now, who brings the news
   who is a tell-tale?
Ainikki, Ahti's sister —
   yes, she brings the news
   she is a tell-tale:
'Darling Ahti my brother!
Kyllikki has been to the village
   within foreign gates
sporting with the village maids

capering with braided heads.'

Ahti boy, the only boy
he, wanton Lemminkäinen
at that was angry, was wroth
   and was long furious.
He himself put this in words:
'O my mother, old woman!
If you were to wash my shirt
   in black snake's venom
and were quickly to dry it
so that I might go to war
to the fires of the North's sons
the grounds of Lapland's children:
Kyllikki has been to the village
   within foreign gates
sporting with the village maids
capering with braided heads.'

And truly Kyllikki says
his wife hastens first to say:
   'My darling Ahti!
   Don't go off to war!
   I dreamed as I lay
   as I soundly slept:
fire like a forge was driving
   flames were flickering
right underneath the window
by the bank at the back wall;
   from there it swirled in
   and like rapids roared
   from floorboards to roof
   window to window.'

There wanton Lemminkäinen
himself put this into words:
'I don't believe women's dreams
   nor the oaths of wives.
O my mother who bore me!
   Bring here my war-gear
   bear my battledress!
   I have a good mind
to go drink the beer of war

to taste the honey of war.'

His mother put this in words:
  'O Ahti my son!
  Don't go off to war!
  We have beer at home
in a barrel of alder
and behind a bung of oak;
I will bring for you to drink
though you were to drink all day.'

Wanton Lemminkäinen said:
'I don't care about home beer!
I would sooner drink river water
off a tarry paddle's blade:
that's sweeter for me to drink
  than all the home brews.
  Bring here my war-gear
  bear my battledress!
I'm off to Northland's cabins
the grounds of Lapland's children
  to lay claim to gold
  to demand silver.'

Lemminkäinen's mother said:
  'Oh, Ahti my son!
  There is gold at home
  silver in our shed.
  Only yesterday
quite early in the morning
a serf ploughed a viper-field
turned over one full of snakes;
the plough lifted a chest lid
its back end raised a penny:
inside hundreds had been stacked
  thousands had been crammed.
I lugged the chest to the shed
put it up in the shed loft.'

Wanton Lemminkäinen said:
'I don't care about home wealth!
If I get one mark from war
I'll regard it as better

than all the home gold
silver lifted by the plough.
Bring here my war-gear
bear my battledress!
I am off to Northland's war
fighting with Lapland's children.

'I have a good mind
and my brain intends
to hear with my ears myself
to see with these eyes of mine
if there's a maid in Northland
a lass in Darkland
who will not accept bridegrooms
not take to good men.'

Lemminkäinen's mother said:
'Oh, Ahti my son!
You have Kyllikki at home
a home-wife that's loftier!
It is grim to have two wives
in one husband's bed.'

Wanton Lemminkäinen said:
'Kyllikki's a gadabout:
let her run in every sport
let her lie in every house
having fun with village girls
capering with braided heads!'

His mother tried to forbid
the old woman warned:
'Just don't, my offspring
don't go to Northland's cabins
unless you are wise
unless you have skill
to the fires of the North's sons
the grounds of Lapland's children!
There a Lapp may sing, a man
of Turja may push your face
into charcoal, your head into clay
into ashes your forearms
your palms into hot cinders

and into burning boulders.'

Lemminkäinen says: 'Witches
have already bewitched me
witches bewitched, vipers cursed;
    three Lapps tested me
    on one summer night
    naked on a rock
    without belt or clothes
    without a stitch on:
    they made out of me
the miserable ones got
what an axe gets from a rock
and an auger from a stone
and a pick from a glacier
death from an empty cabin.

    'Things looked grim one way
but they turned out differently.
They wanted to put me, they
    threatened to sink me
on a swamp for a causeway
for a bridge where there is dirt
to put my chin into slime
my beard into a bad place.
But I, as a special man
did not greatly fret at that;
I became a soothsayer
made myself a spellbinder:
I sang the witches with their arrows
the shooters with their weapons
the sorcerers with their iron knives
and the wise men with their steels
into Tuoni's steep rapids
into the frightful eddy
beneath the highest water-
fall, beneath the worst whirlpool.
There let the witches sleep, there
    let the wicked lie
    until the grass grows
through the head, through the helmet
through a witch's shoulderblades
cleaving the shoulder flesh off

27

a witch where he lies
a wicked man where he sleeps!'

Still his mother banned
Lemminkäinen from going;
the mother forbade her son
and the woman banned her man:
    'Look, just don't go there
    to the cold village
    off to dark Northland!
    Doom at least will come
doom to the worthy boy, ruin
to wanton Lemminkäinen.
Though you speak with a hundred
mouths, I shall still not believe:
there is no singer in you
to match the sons of the North
nor do you know Turja's tongue
and you cannot speak Lappish.'

Then wanton Lemminkäinen
    fair Farmind himself
    was coming his head
    and brushing his hair.
He flung the comb at the wall
the brush he hurled at the post
he uttered a word, spoke thus
himself declared and chattered:
'That will be Lemminkäinen's
ruin, the worthy boy's doom
when the comb is pouring blood
and the brush is babbling gore.'

Wanton Lemminkäinen went
    off to dark Northland
although his mother forbade
    and his parent warned.

    He bolts up, belts up
    puts on iron shirts
    buckles on steel belts.
He himself put this in words:
'In armour a man's tougher

in an iron shirt better
in a steel belt more powerful
amid those witches, so that
he cares not about worse ones
nor yet frets about good ones.'

He took his own sword
   seized his mighty blade
refined among the demons
   ground among the gods;
this he fastens to his side
thrust it into the scabbard.

Where does the man guard himself
the harsh fellow shield himself?
He already guards himself
a bit, harshly shields himself
at the door beneath the beam
by the doorpost of the hut
in the yard where the lane ends
and within the furthest gates.

There the man guarded himself
   against womenfolk;
but that guard was not strong, nor
was the shelter trustworthy
so he further guards himself
   against the menfolk
   where two ways parted
on the back of a blue rock
   upon springy mires
   upon splashing springs
where rapids rushed steeply down
   where great water whirled.

There wanton Lemminkäinen
himself declared and uttered:
'Up from the earth, you swordsmen
fellows as old as the earth
from your wells, you brand-bearers
from your river-graves, bowmen!
Rise, O forest, with your men

all you backwoods with your folk
old mountain-man with your power
water-demon with your ghouls
with your host, water-mistress
water's eldest with your force
maids from every marsh
fine-hemmed from the mires
to assist the only man
to be with the famous boy
that witch-arrows may not pierce
nor a wise man's steel
nor sorcerer's iron knives
no shooter's weapons.

'Should not enough come from that
I recall another way:
higher I will sigh
to that Old Man in the sky
him who keeps the clouds
governs the vapours.

'O Old Man, chief god
old father in heaven
who speak through the clouds
declare down the air!
O bring me a fiery sword
in a fiery sheath, with which
I shall scatter hindrances
and with which I shall break spells
overturn the earth-wicked
conquer water-sorcerers
to the front of me
to the rear of me
above my head, to my side
on both my flanks; I'll impale
the witches on their arrows
the sorcerers on their iron blades
the wise men on their steel blades
the evil men on their swords.'

Then wanton Lemminkäinen
he the fair Farmind
whistled his foal from the copse

from withered grass his gold-maned;
slipped the foal into harness
between shafts his fiery-red.
He himself sat in the sledge
he thudded into his sleigh
   he lashed the courser
goaded with the pebble-tipped.
Courser ran and journey sped
the sledge rolled, the road shortened
   the silver sand rang
   the golden heath boomed.

He went a day, he went two
soon he went a third as well.
   Upon the third day
he comes upon a village.

Then wanton Lemminkäinen
   rumbles on his way
along the outermost road
up to the outermost house.

Over the threshold he asks
spoke from beyond the rooftree:
'Might there be one in this house
who will loosen my breast-straps
   will let down my shafts
unfasten the collar-bow?'

A child declared from the floor
a boy from the staircase end:
'No, there is none in this house
who will loosen your breast-straps
   will let down your shafts
unfasten the collar-bow.'

What did Lemminkäinen care!
   He lashed the courser
whacked it with the beaded belt;
   he rumbles away
along the middlemost road
up to the middlemost house.
Over the threshold he asks

declares from beyond the roof:
'Might there be one in this house
  who will take the reins
  loosen the breast-straps
  pull off the traces?'

A hag scolded from the hearth
a gossip from the stove seat:
'Yes, you'll find some in this house
  who will take your reins
  loosen your breast-straps
  and let down your shafts;
  yes, there are dozens
you'll find (should you want) hundreds
  who'll give you a lift:
they will supply a draft horse
to go, scoundrel, to your home
to flee, villain, to your land
  where your father sits
  where your mother steps
  your brother's gateway
  your sister's floor end
  before the day's out
  and the sun goes down!

What did Lemminkäinen care!
He uttered a word, spoke thus:
  'The hag should be shot
  the hook-chin clobbered.'
He gave the courser its head;
  he swishes away
along the uppermost road
up to the uppermost house.

There wanton Lemminkäinen
as he approaches the house
  he says with this word
  he spoke with this speech:
'Demon, block the barker's mouth
and Devil, the dog's jawbone;
set a block before its mouth
and a gag between its teeth

that it may not make a sound
before the man has gone by!'

So having come to the yard
he smites the earth with his whip:
a mist rose from the whip's path
a little man in the mist;
'twas he loosened the breast-strapes
'twas he who let down the shafts.

Then wanton Lemminkäinen
himself listens with his ears
with nobody spotting him
with no one noticing him:
from outside he heard poems
    through the moss heard words
    through the wall players
and through the shutter singers.

    He glanced in from there
    he peeped secretly:
the cabin was full of clever men
the benches full of singers
the side walls full of players
the doorway of cunning men
the back bench full of wise men
the inglenook of crooners;
they sang poems of Lapland
and a Demon-tale they screeched.

Then wanton Lemminkäinen
dared to become someone else
made bold to transform himself;
from the corner he went in
entered from where the logs joined.
He himself put this in words:
'A song is good when it ends
when 'tis short a tale is fair;
'tis better to keep the thread
than break off in the middle.'

She the mistress of Northland
shifted where the boards joined, paced

33

3

in the middle of the floor.
She uttered a word, spoke thus:
    'A dog has been here
a cur with iron-hued hair
one that eats flesh, that gnaws bones
    that laps up fresh blood.
What kind of man may you be
what sort of fellow are you —
coming into this cabin
getting inside the building
without the dog hearing you
nor the barker noticing?'

Wanton Lemminkäinen said:
'Be sure I did not come here
without my skill, my wisdom
without my might, my knowledge
without my father's magic
and my parent's protection
to be eaten by your dogs
and chopped up by your barkers.

    'My mother washed me
washed me as a little sprout
three times on a summer night
nine times on an autumn night
to be wise on every road
and knowing in every land
to be a singer at home
and a cunning man abroad.'

Then wanton Lemminkäinen
    he the fair Farmind
now became a soothsayer
and turned into a singer:
    his coat hems struck fire
    and his eyes poured flames
as Lemminkäinen sang, as
    he sang and chanted.

He sang the best of singers
into the worst of singers;

rammed rocks sideways in the mouths
piled boulders sidelong in those
    of the best singers
of the most skilful poets.

So he sang the special men
    one this way, one that —
    into treeless glades
    on to unploughed lands
    into fishless pools
    ones quite without perch
into Rutja's steep rapids
into the burning whirlpool
to be foam-crests in the stream
and rocks amid the rapids
    to smoulder as fire
    and to shoot as sparks.

Wanton Lemminkäinen sang
the men thither with their swords
the fellows with their weapons;
he sang the young, sang the old
once he sang one middle-aged;
    one he left unsung —
    a paltry herdsman
an old man, old and sightless.

    Dripcap the herdsman
    put this into words:
'O you wanton Loverboy!
You sang the young, sang the old
once you sang one middle-aged:
so why do you not sing me?'

Wanton Lemminkäinen said:
'Here's why I do not touch you:
you are miserable to look at
wretched without my touching.
When you were a younger man
still, and a paltry herdsman
you ruined your mother's charge
    you raped your sister;
all the horses you disgraced

and the mare's foals you wore out
on open swamp, sunken land
   shifting water-scum.'

   Dripcap the herdsman
at that was angry, furious.
And he went out through the door
to the field across the yard;
ran to Tuonela's river
to the holy stream's whirlpool.
There he looked out for Farmind
he waits for Lemminkäinen
on his way back from Northland
   on his journey home.

The Demon's Elk

Then wanton Lemminkäinen
said to the hag of Northland:
'Hag, now give of your lasses
    bring your girls this way
give me the best of the flock
the tallest of your lass-crowd!'

Well, that mistress of Northland
uttered a word and spoke thus:
'I'll not give you my lasses
nor press upon you my girls
not the best, not the worst, not
the tallest, not the shortest:
you have wedded a wife already
and married a mistress already.'

Wanton Lemminkäinen said:
'I'll tie Kyllikki in the village
to the village threshold steps
to its foreign gates; from here
I will get a better wife.
Now bring your daughter this way
the finest of the maid-flock
fairest of the braided heads!'

The mistress of Northland said:
'No, I will not give my girl
   to a worthless man
a good-for-nothing fellow.
   Only beg for girls
sue for flower-heads when you have
skied after the Demon's elk
brought it from his fields' far ends!'

Then wanton Lemminkäinen
fitted ferrules on his spears
   strung up his crossbows
   and prepared his bolts.
He himself put this in words:
'The spear may have a ferrule
all the bolts may be ready
the bow supplied with a string
but there's no left ski to push
no right for the heel to smite.'

There wanton Lemminkäinen
   thinks and considers
from where he might get snowshoes
from whom a mere hint of skis.

He went to Kauppi's farm, he
stopped at Lyylikki's smithy:
   'O shrewd Gothlander
   fair Kauppi the Lapp!
Make me fine skis, gouge fair ones
right and left, on which I may
ski after the Demon's elk
bring it from his fields' far ends!'

And Lyylikki says a word
Kauppi puts in with his tongue:
'Vainly, Lemminkäinen, you
go to hunt the Demon's elk:
you will get a scrap of rotten wood
and even that with great grief.'

What did Lemminkäinen care!
He himself put this in words:

'Make me a left ski to push
a right ski to shove! I shall
ski after the elk, bring it
from the Demon's fields' far ends.'

Lyylikki, smith of left skis
Kauppi, maker of right skis
all autumn shaped a left ski
all winter gouged a right ski
all day he cut a pole shaft
all next put on a snow-disc.

The left ski was fit to push
the right for the heel to smite
and the pole shafts were ready
and the snow-discs were put on.
A pole shaft cost an otter
and a snow-disc a brown fox.

With butter he greased his skis
smeared them with reindeer tallow;
    and at that he thinks
    he says with this word:
'Might there among these youngsters
among the growing folk be
any to push this left ski
of mine, to heel-kick the right?'

Wanton Lemminkäinen said
the full-blooded rogue uttered:
'Indeed among these youngsters
among the growing folk there
are some to push this left ski
of yours, to heel-kick the right.'

A quiver he fastened on his back
on his shoulder a new bow
grasped the pole shaft in his hand;
he went to push the left ski
    to heel-kick the right.
He himself put this in words:
    'Surely in God's air
beneath the lid of this sky
there's nothing in the forest

running on four feet
that's not taken by surprise
handsomely carried off, with
the skis of Kaleva's son
with Lemminkäinen's sliders.'

And the Demons got to hear
the judases to take note.
And the Demons built an elk
the judases a reindeer:
they make a head of a block
antlers of goat-willow forks
    and feet of driftwood
and legs of stakes from a swamp
    a back of wattles
and sinews of dry grasses
and eyes of pond lily buds
and ears of pond lily flowers
    and skin of spruce bark
other flesh of rotten wood.

The Demon advised his elk
to his reindeer spoke by mouth:
'Now run, you elk of Demons
    foot it, noble deer
to where the reindeer breeds, to
the grounds of Lapland's children!
Make a man ski till he sweats —
Lemminkäinen most of all!'

At that the Demon's elk ran
the wild reindeer trotted off
below the North's sheds and through
the grounds of Lapland's children:
it kicked a tub from a hut
it knocked the pans off the fire
spoilt the meat in the ashes
spilt broth all over the hearth.

    Quite a din rose on
the grounds of Lapland's children —
    Lapland's dogs barking
and Lapland's children crying

and Lapland's women laughing
and other people grumbling!
He, wanton Lemminkäinen
kept skiing after the elk.
He skied on swamps, skied on lands
he skied upon open glades:
    fire swished from the skis
smoke from the tips of the poles;
but he did not see his elk
    neither saw nor heard.

He slid up hill, slid down dale
slid through lands beyond the sea;
skied through all the Demon's woods
all the heaths of Death as well
skied before the mouth of Doom
and behind the farm of Death.

    Doom opens its mouth
    and Death leans its head
    to take the fellow
to swallow Lemminkäinen:
but it missed him by a mile
    did not stand a chance.

A strip was yet unslid through
a corner of woods untouched
at the North's far distant end
    in open Lapland.
He went to slide through that too
to touch that corner of woods.

Reaching his destination
    he heard quite a din
at the North's far distant end
the grounds of Lapland's children:
    he heard dogs barking
and Lapland's children crying
and Lapland's women laughing
and the other Lapps grumbling.

Then wanton Lemminkäinen
forthwith went skiing that way

to where the dogs were barking
the grounds of Lapland's children.

He said having arrived there
   inquired having come:
'Why did the women laugh here
women laugh and children cry
   the old people groan
what did the watchdogs bark at?'

'Here's why the women laughed here
women laughed and children cried
   the old people groaned
here's what the watchdogs barked at:
the Demons' elk ran this way
   the smooth-hoof galloped;
it kicked a tub from a hut
it knocked the pans off the fire
it tipped the soup upside down
spilt gruel all over the hearth.'

At that the full-blooded rogue
that wanton Lemminkäinen
pushed his left ski on the snow
like a viper in the grass
and made his swamp-pine slither
   like a snake alive;
he uttered as he careered
   said with pole in hand:
'What men there are in Lapland
all will carry off the elk;
   what women there are
   all will wash their pots;
   what children there are
   all will gather wood;
   and what pots there are
   all will cook the elk!'

He made fast, he tensed himself
he kicked off, he took the strain.
   The first time, he kicked
until no eye could spot him;
   the next time, he thrust

until no ear could hear him;
   the third, he speeds on
the tail of the Demons' elk.

He took a maple tether
he grabbed a birch withe, with which
he tied up the Demons' elk
   inside an oak pen:
   'Stay there, Demons' elk
   wild reindeer, trot there!'

   And he strokes its back
   and he pats its hide:
   'Would I might stay here
it would suit me to lie down
   beside a young maid
   with a growing hen!'

Then the Demon's elk flared up
the wild reindeer started to
kick, it uttered, this it says:
'The devil fix it for you
   to lie with young maids
   to live with daughters!'

It took the strain, tensed itself:
   the birch withe it tore
it snapped the maple tether
   the oak pen it smashed.
   Then it wandered off
   the elk skipped away
towards swamps and towards lands
   to a bushy hill
until no eye could spot it
until no ear could hear it.

And there the full-blooded rogue
   was angry and wroth
sorely angry and furious.
He skied off after the elk;
but with one kick the left ski
bent in half at the toe hole
the ski gave at the foot plate

the right ski broke by the heel
the spear where the ferrule was
the pole at the snow-disc joint.
The Demon's elk itself ran
so that its head was not seen.

There wanton Lemminkäinen
his head down, in bad spirits
   gazes at his things.
He himself put this in words:
   'Never, nevermore
may another of our men
rashly go forest hunting
ski after the Demon's elk
as I, luckless one, have gone!
I have destroyed good showshoes
and a fair pole I have lost
and the sharpest of my spears!'

Elk, Horse, Swan

Then wanton Lemminkäinen
   thought and considered
upon which path he should press
along which trail he should go:
should he leave the Demon's elks
   and make his way home
or should he keep on trying
   skiing at his ease
to please the forest mistress
to delight the backwoods girls?

   He says with this word
   he spoke with this speech:
   'O Old Man, chief god
   heavenly father!
   Make me now straight skis
   light ones, left and right
on which I may ski along
across swamps and across lands
ski towards the Demon's lands
across the heaths of the North
to where the Demon's elk roams
the wild reindeer's stamping grounds!

'I go from men forestward
from fellows to outdoor work
along Tapiola's roads
and through Tapio's houses.
    Hail, mountains, hail, hills
    hail, soughing spruces
    hail, pale green aspens
    hail one who hails you!

'Soften, forest, be kind, woods
incline, precious Tapio!
See a man to the island
    lead him to that knoll
where a catch is to be made
and prey to be caught and brought!

'Nyyrikki, Tapio's son
clear-skinned man, red-helmeted!
Cut marks all along the lands
    put signs in the hills
that this fool may feel the way
and this stranger know the road
    as I seek prey, as
    I beg for a gift!

'Mielikki, forest mistress
clear-skinned crone, fair of feature!
    Set gold in motion
    silver wandering
in front of the man seeking
in the steps of one who begs!

    'Take golden keys from
    the ring at your thigh
and open Tapio's shed
and shift the forest's stronghold
on the days of my hunting
at the times of my prey-search!

'Should you not care to yourself
    then make your lasses
    compel your hirelings
order those who take orders!

46

Surely you are no mistress
if you do not keep a maid
  keep a hundred maids
a thousand order-takers
guardians of all your stock
cherishers of all your wealth.
  'Tiny forest lass
mead-mouthed maid of Tapio!
Play a honey-sweet whistle
pipe on a mead-sweet whistle
in the ear of the graceful
the pleasant forest mistress
  that she may soon hear
  and rise from her bed
for she does not hear at all
  hardly ever wakes
  though I keep begging
beseech with a golden tongue!'

Then wanton Lemminkäinen
  all the time gameless
skied on swamps and skied on lands
  skied through hard backwoods
  on God's charcoal hills
on the Demon's coal-black heaths.

He skied a day, he skied two.
  Now on the third day
  he climbed a great hill
  rose on a great rock
  moved his eyes north-west
  across swamps northward:
Tapio's houses appeared
  the golden doors loomed
from across a swamp northward
from under a hill, from scrub.

That wanton Lemminkäinen
  straight away drew near
  came close and arrived
beneath Tapio's window.
  He crouched down to look
  through the sixth window:

there the givers dwelt
and the wealth-dames stretched
in plain working clothes
in dirty tatters.

Wanton Lemminkäinen said:
'Why, forest mistress, do you
dwell in working clothes
in kiln-rags wallow
thoroughly black of feature
grim of appearance
wicked of aspect
your frame ugly to behold?

'When I walked through the forest
there were three strongholds —
one of wood and one of bone
and the third a stone stronghold;
six golden windows
were at each stronghold's corner.
I peered in through these
as I stood below the wall:
the master and the mistress
of Tapio's house
Tellervo, Tapio's maid
and with them Tapio's other folk
were all swarming dressed in gold
sauntering dressed in silver.
The forest mistress herself
the gracious forest mistress
had hands swathed in gold
fingers in gold rings
head adorned with gold
her hair coiled with gold
ears dangling with gold
her neck with good beads.

'Sweet forest mistress
Forestland's honey-sweet crone!
Cast off your haymaking shoes
shed your birchbark burning-shoes
take off your kiln-rags
drop your working-shirt!

Dress in lucky clothes
put on shirts for game
on the days of my stalking
at the times of my prey-search!
I fill with boredom
fill up with boredom
in this idleness
at all this time without game
for at no time do you give
hardly ever look after.
Boring the joyless evening
long the day without a catch.

'Old forest greybeard
sprig-hatted, lichen-coated!
Dress the forests in linens
clothe the backwoods in broadcloth
the aspens all in jackets
the alders in their best clothes!
In silver deck out the firs
set up the spruces in gold
the old firs in copper belts
and the pines in silver belts
the birches in golden flowers
the stumps in golden trinkets!
Dress them as in ancient times
in your better days:
like the moon the spruce boughs shone
and like the sun the pine tops
the forest smelt of honey
and of mead the blue backwoods
the glade edges of wort, swamp
edges of melted butter.

'Forest girl, sweet maid
Tuulikki, daughter of Tapio!
Drive the wealth towards the slopes
into the most open glades!
If it be stiff in running
or lazy in galloping
take a lash from the thicket
a birch from the woody dell
with which to tickle its flank

49

4

and prod its armpits!
Let it run swiftly
and quickly hasten
in front of the man seeking
in the steps of one who plods!

'When the wealth reaches the track
goad it up the track!
Form with your two palms
a rail on two sides
that the wealth may not dodge past
sheer away from the roadside!
But if the wealth does dodge past
sheer away from the roadside
bring it roadward by the ears
see it by the horns trackward!

'A trunk lies across the road:
just push it aside;
trees on the ground in the way —
break them into two!

'It will come upon a fence:
knock the fence askew
leaving a space five withes high
and seven stakes wide!

'A river will confront it
a brook flow across the road:
seize silk for a bridge
red broadcloth for steps!
Get across the straits as well
and drag across the waters
and across Northland's river
over where the rapids foam!

'Master of Tapio's house
mistress of Tapio's house
old forest greybeard
golden forest king!
Mimerkki, forest mistress
kind and giving forest crone
blue-cloaked thicket dame
red-socked swamp mistress!

Come now to change gold
to barter silver!
My gold is old as the moon
and the sun's age my silver
gained defiantly from war
threateningly from battle;
but coins wear out in a purse
darken in a tinder box
when there's no one to change gold
to barter silver.'

So wanton Lemminkäinen
for days skied along
sang tales at a thicket top
three in a woody hollow:
he pleased the forest mistress
and the forest master too
he delighted all the girls
persuaded Tapio's maids.

They chased, they hounded
the Demon's elk from its hiding place
round behind Tapio's hill
from the bounds of the Demon's stronghold
in front of the seeking man
for the spellbinder to claim.

He, wanton Lemminkäinen
let fly his lassoo
at the shoulders of the Demon's elk
the neck of the camel-colt
so that it did not kick wickedly
when he stroked its back.

Then wanton Lemminkäinen
himself put this into words:
'Lord of the woods, land master
fair one living on the heath!
Mielikki, forest mistress
kind and giving forest crone!
Come now, take the gold
and choose the silver!
Put your linen on the ground

spread out your best flaxen stuff
underneath the gleaming gold
and the glittering silver
   unspilled on the ground
   unsoiled in the dirt!'

Then he set out for Northland;
and he said having come there:
'I have skied and caught the Demon's elk
at the far end of the Demon's fields.
   Hag, give me your girl
   give me the young bride!'

Louhi, mistress of Northland
   this one answered that:
'I'll only give my daughter
   and the young bride, when
you bridle the great gelding
   the Demon's brown horse
the Demon's foal whose jaw foams
at the far end of the Demon's turfs.'

Then wanton Lemminkäinen
   took his golden reins
   his silver bit-chain;
he goes to search for the horse
to listen for the flax-mane
at the far end of the Demon's turfs.
   And he trips along
   he bowls on his way
   to the green meadow
   the holy field's edge.
   There he seeks the horse
listens for the flaxen one
a yearling's bit at his belt
shouldering a foal's harness.

He sought a day, he sought two
   and on the third day
   he climbed a great hill
clambered upon a rock's back;
he cast his eyes southward, turned
his head to beneath the sun:

on the sand he saw the horse
the flax-mane among spruces;
   its hair flashed with fire
   its mane billows smoke.

Lemminkäinen says:
   'O Old Man, chief god
Old Man, keeper of the clouds
governor of the vapours!
   Open up the sky
all the air into windows!
   Send iron hailstones
   drop icy coolers
on the mane of the good horse
on the sides of the Demon's blaze-head!'

That Old Man, chief creator
   god above the clouds
rent the air into a rage
   the sky's lid in two;
   he rained slush, rained ice
   he rained iron hail
smaller than a horse's head
but bigger than a man's head
on the mane of the good horse
on the sides of the Demon's blaze-head.

Then wanton Lemminkäinen
   went over to look
   to inspect closely.
And he put this into words:
'O good horse of Demonland
mountain foal of foaming jaw!
Put now your golden muzzle
   slip your silver head
   into golden rings
   into silver bells!
I may not treat you badly
or drive you quite so sternly:
I'll drive you a tiny way
a very little journey
thither to Northland's cabins
to a harsh mother-in-law.

What I shall slap with a thong
   or smack with a lash
   I shall slap with silk
   smack with a cloth hem.'

   The Demon's brown horse
the Demon's foal whose jaw foams
pushed then its golden muzzle
   slipped its silver head
   into golden rings
   into silver bells.

Well, wanton Lemminkäinen
now bridled the great gelding
slipped the bit into its golden mouth
his bridle over its silver head;
he leapt on the good one's back
on the sides of the Demon's blaze-head.

   He lashed the courser
thrashed it with a willow switch.
He drove a little journey
   cantered up a fell
up the north side of a hill
   up a snowy slope:
he came to Northland's cabins.
He went indoors from the yard
   said having come there
   having reached Northland:
'I've bridled the great gelding
the Demon's foal I've harnessed
brought it from the green meadow
   the holy field's edge
and I've skied after the Demon's elk
brought it from the Demon's fields' far end.
So now, hag, give me your girl
   give me the young bride!'

Louhi, mistress of Northland
well, she put this into words:
'I'll only give my daughter
   the young bride when you
shoot the swan on the river

on the stream the splendid fowl
upon Tuoni's black river
on the holy stream's whirlpool
   at a single try
raising a single arrow.'

Then wanton Lemminkäinen
   he the fair Farmind
went to the swan's droning, to
look for the long-neck, bring it
out of Tuoni's black river
from the dale of the Dead Land.

And he swings along
   hurries on his way
towards Tuonela's river
to the holy stream's whirlpool
shouldering his handsome bow
a quiverful on his back.

Dripcap the herdsman
the old blind man of Northland
is at Tuonela's river
at the holy stream's whirlpool;
   he looks, he turns round
for Lemminkäinen's coming.

One day among others he
saw wanton Lemminkäinen
arriving and coming close
there at Tuonela's river
beside the wrathful rapids
at the holy stream's whirlpool.

He raised up a water snake
a cowbane out of the waves
plunged it right through the man's heart
through Lemminkäinen's liver
and right through his left armpit
into his right shoulderblade.

Now wanton Lemminkäinen
   felt it hurting hard.

He uttered a word, spoke thus:
    'I did the worst work
not remembering to ask
my mother, her who bore me
    for but two small words
(hardly many even three)
how to be, which way to live
    in these evil days:
I don't know the hurts of water snakes
    the pains of cowbane.

'O my mother who bore me
woe-witness who cared for me!
    If you knew or felt
    where your poor son is
of course you would come dashing
you'd be in time to help me;
    you'd take your poor son
off this road away from death
from falling asleep while young
from passing while full-blooded.'

Then the blind one of Northland
    Dripcap the herdsman
plunged wanton Lemminkäinen
felled the son of Kaleva
into Tuoni's black river
down into the worst whirlpool.
Wanton Lemminkäinen went
over the rapids roaring
with the current flickering
towards Tuonela's cabins.

That bloody son of Tuoni
struck at the man with his sword
    slashed him with his blade.
With one flashing stroke he smote
    the man in five bits
into eight pieces, tossed him
into Tuonela's river
into the Dead Land's eddies:
    'Stretch there for ever
with your crossbow, your arrows!

Shoot the swans on the river
the waterfowl on the banks!'

That was Lemminkäinen's end
the death of the stern suitor
down in Tuoni's black river
in the dale of the Dead Land.

Resurrection

The wanton Lemminkäinen's
mother at home keeps thinking:
'Where's Lemminkäinen got to
where has my Farmind vanished?
For no one hears him coming
from his travels in the world.'

The poor mother does not know
nor does the wretch who bore him
know where her flesh is moving
where her own blood is rolling
whether on a cone-clad hill
on heather-covered heathland
or upon the open sea
   on the foam-capped waves
   or in a great war
   a dreadful revolt
in which blood reaches the shin
   redness is knee-deep.

Kyllikki the handsome wife
looks about and turns about
in wanton Lemminkäinen's
home, on Farmind's farm. She looked
in the evening at his comb

in the morning at his brush;
on a day among others
a morning among many
blood was leaking from the comb
gore was oozing from the brush.

Kyllikki the handsome wife
uttered a word and spoke thus:
'Now my man has gone from me
may fair Farmind has vanished
on travels without shelter
    and on unknown roads:
blood is leaking from the comb
gore is oozing from the brush!'

Then Lemminkäinen's mother
herself looks upon the comb
herself gave way to weeping:
'Alas, poor me, for my days
afflicted one, for my times!
    Now my son, poor me,
now, hapless me, my offspring
has come upon evil days!
Doomed my worthy son, ruined
the wanton Lemminkäinen:
now the comb is pouring blood
and the brush is dripping gore!'

In her fists she grasped her hems
    in her arms her clothes.
Soon she ran a long journey
    she both ran and rushed:
she pounded hills as she went
raised marshes and flattened fells
    highlands she brought low
    lowlands she lifted.

She came to Northland's cabins.
    She asked for her son
    she asked, she inquired:
'O you mistress of Northland!
Where have you taken Lemminkäinen?
Which way did you send my son?'

Louhi, mistress of Northland
    this one answered that:
'I know nothing of your son
where he has gone and vanished.
I sat him in a stallion's
sledge, a most fiery one's sleigh;
could he have drowned in slush, gone
    solid on sea ice
or got into the wolf's mouth
the jaws of the dreadful bear?'

Lemminkäinen's mother said:
'You have told nothing but lies!
A wolf will not eat my kin
no bear fells Lemminkäinen:
with his fingers he crushes
wolves, with his hands he fells bears.
    If you do not tell
where you have taken Lemminkäinen
I will smash the new kiln's door
and break the Sampo's hinges.'

The mistress of Northland said:
    'I fed the man full
    let him drink his fill
fed him till he was drowsy;
I sat him in a boat's stern
    made him shoot rapids.
But I cannot imagine
where the poor wretch has got to —
whether in foaming rapids
    or in swirling streams.'

Lemminkäinen's mother said:
'You have told nothing but lies!
    Tell the truth with care
    have told your last lies
where you have taken Lemminkäinen
doomed the Kalevala man
or 'twill be the death of you
    you will meet your end!'

The mistress of Northland said:
'Suppose now I tell the truth:

I set him skiing for elk
  skinning noble beasts
  bridling great geldings
  and harnessing foals;
I made him search for the swan
  hunt the holy fowl.
Now I cannot imagine
what has come by way of doom
turned up by way of hindrance
for no one hears him coming
  to hunt for a bride
  to beg for a girl.'

The mother seeks the one strayed
for the vanished one she longs.
She ran great swamps as a wolf
trod backwoods as a bruin
waters as an otter ranged
lands she walked as a black ant
as a wasp headland borders
  as a hare lakeshores.
  Rocks she shoved aside
  and roots she tilted
moved dead boughs to the roadside
kicked dead trunks to form causeways.

For long she seeks the one strayed
for long seeks but does not find.
She asked the trees for her son
she longed for her one vanished.
A tree talked, a fir tree sighed
an oak skilfully answered:
'I have cares of my own too
with no cares about your son
for I was formed for hard times
was put here for evil days —
to be chopped up for stacking
to be cut down for firewood
to sicken for drying-wood
to be felled for slash and burn.'

For long she seeks the one strayed
for long seeks and does not find.

She comes upon a small road;
    to the road she bows:
'O small road, God's creature! Have
    you not seen my son
    my apple of gold
    my staff of silver?'

The road skilfully answered
it both declared and chattered:
'I have cares of my own too
with no cares about your son
for I was formed for hard times
was put here for evil days —
for every dog to run on
every horseman to ride on
every hard shoe to walk on
    every heel to scrape.'

For long she seeks the one strayed
for long seeks but does not find.
And she comes upon the moon;
    to the moon she bows:
'Precious moon, God's creature! Have
    you not seen my son
    my apple of gold
    my staff of silver?'

That moon, God's creature
skilfully enough answered:
'I have cares of my own too
with no cares about your son
for I was formed for hard times
was put here for evil days —
to travel the nights alone
    to shine in the frost
to keep watch over winters
to vanish for the summer.'

For long she seeks the one strayed
for long seeks but does not find.
And she comes upon the sun;
    to the sun she bows:
'O sun, creature of God! Have
    you not seen my son

my apple of gold
my staff of silver?'

Well now, the sun knew something
    the daylight worked out:
    'Your son, poor you, has
    been lost, has been killed
down in Tuoni's black river
the Dead Land's ageless water —
over the rapids roaring
with the current flickering
towards Tuonela's far ends
to the dales of the Dead Land.'

Then Lemminäinen's mother
herself burst into weeping.
She went to the place of smiths:
    'Smith Ilmarinen!
You forged once, forged yesterday
    now forge this day too!
    Helve a copper rake
fit it with prongs of iron;
forge prongs a hundred fathoms
long, prepare a shaft of five!'

    Smith Ilmarinen
the everlasting craftsman
    helved a copper rake
fitted with prongs of iron;
forged prongs a hundred fathoms
long, prepared a shaft of five.

She, Lemminkäinen's mother
    gets the iron rake
flew to Tuonela's river.
    She implores the sun:
'O sun, god's creature, creature
of the Creator, our light!
Shine for a moment sultry
another dimly swelter
and a third with all your might;
put the weary folk to sleep
tire the crowd of the Dead Land

wear down the host of Tuoni!'

That sun, God's creature, creature
of the Creator, daylight
flew on to a crooked birch
to a warped alder it flapped.
It shone a moment sultry
another dimly sweltered
and a third with all its might
put the weary folk to sleep
tired the crowd of the Dead Land
the young men upon their swords
and the old against their sticks
the middle-aged on their spears.
    Then it slouched away
to the top of level heaven
to where it had been before
    the room it once had.

Then Lemminkäinen's mother
    took the iron rake;
    she rakes for her son
among the foaming rapids
    the flickering stream.
She rakes but she does not find.

Then she shifted further down —
went all the way to the sea
up to her sock-string in wet
up to her waist in water.

    She rakes for her son
along Tuonela's river
she dredges against the stream.
She dragged once, and for that twice:
she gets only her son's shirt
the shirt much to her distress;
she dragged yet another time:
she got socks, a hat she found —
    socks to her great grief
    hat to her dismay.

From there she stepped still further
to the dales of the Dead Land

dragged once along the water
a second time across the water
a third squintwise across the water.
    Now, at the third time
a mass of entrails came forth
    on the iron rake.

Mass of entrails it was not:
'twas wanton Lemminkäinen
    he the fair Farmind
stuck on the prongs of the rake
stuck by his nameless finger
    stuck by his left toe.

Wanton Lemminkäinen rose
and Kaleva's son came up
    on the copper rake
on top of the clear waters;
only... a bit was missing —
    one hand, half his head
and many other gobbets
    and no breath either.

    There his mother thinks
    and weeping she says:
'Could a man still come of this
a new fellow recover?'

A raven happened to hear.
    This one answers that:
'There is no man in one gone
    in one come to grief:
now the whitefish has eaten his eyes
the pike has split his shoulders.
Just let the man go into the sea
push him into Tuonela's river!
Perhaps he'll become a cod
    flourish as a whale.'

That Lemminkäinen's mother
    does not push her son.
    She dredges once more
    with the copper rake

along Tuonela's river
along as well as across:
she gets some hand, gets some head
she gets half of a back-bone
the other half of a rib
many another gobbet.
Out of them she built a son
made wanton Lemminkäinen.

She joined flesh to flesh
bones to bones she slid
and limbs to their limbs
sinews to sinew fractures.

She herself bound up sinews
she tied up ends of sinews
and the yarn of sinews she
tells over, saying these words:
'Gracious mistress of sinews
Sinew-daughter, gracious dame
dainty spinner of sinews
with the gracious spinning-tool
the copper spindle
and the iron wheel!
Come here when you are needed
walk this way when you are called
a bundle of sinews in your arms
a ball of membranes under your arm
to bind up sinews
to tie up ends of sinews
in the wounds that are cloven
in the gashes that are torn!

'Should not enough come of that
there's a maid above the air
with a copper boat
with a red-sterned craft.
Come, maid, from above the air
maiden, from the pole of heaven!
Row the boat down the sinews
shake it down the limbs
row through gaps in bone
and through cracks in limbs!

'Put the sinews in their place
and set them in their setting —
face to face the great sinews
the arteries eye to eye
overlapping set the veins
the small sinews end to end!

'Then take up a fine needle
a silk thread through the needle!
  Sew with fine needles
  with tin needles stitch
and tie up ends of sinews
with silken ribbons bind them!

'Should not enough come of that
you yourself, god of the air
  harness up your foals
  make ready your steeds!
  Drive with your bright sleigh
  through bone and through limb
  through loose flesh and through
  slippery sinews!
  Join bone up to flesh
sinew up to sinew end
  silver the gapped bone
  gild the crushed sinew!

'Where a membrane is broken
  make a membrane grow
  where sinew is crushed
  tie up a sinew
  where blood has been spilt
  make the blood ripple
  where bone is shattered
  slide bone together
  where the flesh is loose
  join flesh together
and bless it into its place
and set it in its setting —
bone to bone and flesh to flesh
  and limbs to their limbs!'

Thus Lemminkäinen's mother
formed the man, shaped the fellow

to the life he had before
to the features he once had.

She had the sinews all told
the ends of the sinews bound
but had not the man talking
    not her child speaking.

Then she put this into words
herself declared and spoke thus:
'Whence now may ointment be had
and a drop of mead be brought
to anoint the weary one
make the ill-befallen well
that the man may find his words
    return to his tales?

   'O bee, bird of ours
   king of forest flowers!
   Go now, fetch honey
   go and bring back mead
out of pleasant Forestland
from careful Tapiola
from the heads of many flowers
the husks of many grasses
to be ointment for the sick
   to make the ill well!'

The bee, the brisk bird
    forthwith fluttered off
into pleasant Forestland
to careful Tapiola.
It pecked flowers on the meadow
cooked honey upon its tongue
    from six flower-tips, from
    a hundred grass-husks.
    So it comes panting
    it shuffles along
all its wings drenched in mead, its
feathers in melted honey.

She, Lemminkäinen's mother
took up those ointments, with them

anointed the weary one
made the ill-befallen well;
but no help came out of them
and no words came to the man.

Then she put this into words:
　'Bee, my little bird!
　Fly that other way
　right over nine seas
to an island in the sea
　a honeyed mainland
　to Thor's new cabin
the Worshipful's boundless one!

There is pleasant honey there
　and good ointment there
　which will suit sinews
　and be good for limbs.
　So bring those ointments
　bear those remedies
for me to put on the hurt
to pour on the injury!'

　The bee, lightweight man
　again flitted off
　right over nine seas
　half a tenth sea too.
It flew a day, it flew two
soon it flew a third as well
without sitting on a reed
without resting on a leaf
to an island in the sea
　a honeyed mainland
to a mighty rapid's brink
to a holy stream's whirlpool.

　There honey was cooked
　salves were made ready
　in tiny cauldrons
　in fair cooking-pans
　that would hold a thumb
　fit a fingertip.

　The bee, lightweight man

went for those ointments.
A short time passes
a moment speeds by:
now it comes buzzing
it arrives bustling
six cups in its arms
seven on its back —
they're full of ointments
and full of good salves.

She, Lemminkäinen's mother
anointed with those ointments
  with the nine ointments
  the eight remedies:
  still she got no help —
  no, found none from it.

  So she said these words
  and she spoke this speech:
  'Bee, bird of the air!
  Fly there a third time
  high up into heaven
  above nine heavens!
There is mead in plenty there
honey to the heart's content
with which the Lord recited
  the pure God pronounced
the Lord anointed his brood
injured by an evil power.
Wet your wings with mead, and your
feathers with melted honey
  bring mead on your wing
and bear honey on your cloak
to be ointment for the sick
to pour on the injury!'

  The bee, kindly bird
  managed to put this in words:
  'But how am I to get there —
  I a man of little strength?'

  'You will get there easily
    trip there handsomely

over the moon, underneath
the sun, between heaven's stars.
For a day you will flutter
   to the moon's brow-bones
for another you will whizz
to the Great Bear's shoulder-blades
for a third you will rise up
on to the Seven Stars' back;
then 'tis a scrap of a way
   a tiny circuit
to where God the holy lives
to the blessed one's dwellings.'

And the bee rose from the earth
the mead-wing from a hummock;
   now it fluttered off
   whizzed on little wings.
It flew beside the moon's rim
the sun's border it skirted
past the Great Bear's shoulder-blades
the back of the Seven Stars:
it flew to the Lord's cellar
to the almighty's chamber.
   There ointment is made
   salves are made ready
   in pots of silver
   and in pans of gold:
honey boiled in the middle
at the brims melted butter
   mead high in the south
   salves down in the north.

   The bee, the air bird
   then got enough mead
honey to the heart's content.
   A little time passed:
   now it comes panting
   it arrives shuffling
with a hundred hornfuls in its arms
a thousand other bulges —
in them honey and water
within them the best ointment.

Then Lemminkäinen's mother

took them into her own mouth
and tested them with her tongue
　and tasted them well:
　'These are those ointments
the almighty's remedies
with which God has anointed
the Lord poured on injuries.'

Then she anointed the weary one
made the ill-befallen well —
anointed through gaps in bone
　and through cracks in limbs
anointed below, above
　slapped the middle once.
Then she put this into words
herself declared and chattered:
　'Rise up out of sleep
　get up out of dream
up from these evil places
up from the bed of hard luck!'

And the man rose out of sleep
　he woke out of dream.
Now he manages to say
himself to tell with his tongue:
'Ages this wretch has slumbered
long this luckless one has slept!
　I've slept a sweet sleep
a sound one I have enjoyed.'

Lemminkäinen's mother said
herself declared and chattered:
'You would have slept longer still
yet more ages would have lain
but for your evil mother
for the mean one who bore you.

　'Say now, my poor boy
tell so that my ears may hear:
what brought you to the Dead Land
pushed you into Tuonela's river?'

Wanton Lemminkäinen said

answered his mother:
'Dripcap the herdsman
Dreamland's sightless one —
he brought me to the Dead Land
pushed me into Tuonela's river.
He raised a snake out of the water
a dragon out of the waves
    against hapless me;
and I did not know of it
did not know the wrath of water snakes
    the pains of cowbane.'

Lemminkäinen's mother said:
'Alas for a stupid man!
You boasted of bewitching
witches, of singing at Lapps
but don't know the wrath of water snakes
    the pains of cowbane!
From water the water snake was born
and the cowbane from the waves
from the long-tailed duck's good brains
inside the sea-swallow's head.
On the waters the Ogress
spat, dropped a blob on the waves;
the water stretched it out long
the sun shone till it was soft.
*   Then the wind lulled it*
and the water's breath rocked it;
billows washed it to the shore
and the swell steered it to land.'

Then Lemminkäinen's mother
   lulled the one she knew
   to his former state
to the features he once had
till he was a bit better
more graceful than formerly.
   Then she asked her son
was he short of anything?

Wanton Lemminkäinen said:
'There's a lot I'm still short of:
   there my heart's desire

there my longing lies —
with those maidens of the North
   those fair braided heads.
The mould-eared dame of the North
   will not give her girl
till I shoot the long-tailed duck
   till I hit the swan
on that Tuonela river
on the holy stream's whirlpool.'

Lemminkäinen's mother said
herself declared and chattered:
   'Leave your damned swans, let
   the long-tailed ducks be
upon Tuoni's black river
   the smoking whirlpool!
   You just come home now
   with your mean mother!
   And still thank your luck
   your God known to all
for giving you real help
and bringing you back to life
from Tuoni's undoubted road
the abode of the Dead Land!
   I could do nothing
   nothing by myself
without the mercy of God
the guidance of the true Lord.'

Then wanton Lemminkäinen
   quickly set off home
   with his dear mother
beside his honoured parent.

There now I lose my Farmind
leave wanton Lemminkäinen
out of my tale for some time;
and I turn my tale meanwhile
I let my song go elsewhere
I push on to a new track.

Keith Bosley

is an English poet,
translator, and broadcaster.
He is now working on a new
English translation of the *Kalevala*.
   Keith Bosley was born
in the Thames Valley in 1937
and attended the universities
of Reading, Paris and Caen
and graduated in French.
He works for the BBC External Services,
and lives in Slough near London.
He is the author of four
volumes of poetry, and many volumes
of verse translation from
more than forty languages.
His latest collection is *Stations* (1979).
His translations include
an anthology of Vietnamese poetry
The War Wife (1972),
The Song of Songs (1976),
Mallarmé: The Poems (1977),
Eino Leino: Whitsongs (1978),
The Elek Book of Oriental Verse (1979),
and *From the Theorems of
Master Jean de la Ceppéde* (1982).
He has received first prize in two recent
translation competitions.
   Keith Bosley's interest
in Finnish folk poetry dates back
more than twenty years.

He translated and
edited prose stories
from the *Kalevala* under
the title *Tales from the Long Lakes* 1966,
which has also been translated into Dutch.
In 1973 he published a translation
of the famous Aino poem from the *Kalevala*.
Outstanding among Keith Bosley's
translations from Finnish is
Finnish Folk Poetry, Epic 1977.
He was awarded the Finnish State
Prize for Translators in 1978.

From Keith Bosley's
Finnish Notebook

Lieksa, North Karelia
(1974, unpublished)

The mistress's domain:
at a small window
a spinning-wheel
with flax on its distaff

a dresser full of plates, cups
and spoons carved with joy
the fingers feel it still
                              a bench
runs round the wall
to another window
where it joins chairs
set at a long table for a meal

from a peg in the corner
a *kantele* hangs
                    unstrung
the high rafters reflect
only the thud of boots
the stove is cold by the door

in such a place
a blind singer, good
for no other work
opened his locks of bone
unrolled his wisdom.